Owls are often portrayed as being wise and magical birds. This is possibly because they are often alone; they are mainly nocturnal (which means that they are awake at night); and they can fly noiselessly thanks to the shape of their wing feathers.

There are about two hundred different types of owl. Owls are found on all of the continents except Antarctica.

feathers

barn owl

Snowy owls have thick feathers – even on their feet! These feathers keep them snug in the freezing Arctic weather. The males' feathers are white, which makes them difficult to see against a snowy landscape.

male snowy owl

Snowy owls are around 70cm tall. Their wingspan can be as much as 1.5m.

Snowy owls hunt small animals, such as lemmings. They swoop down and grab them with their strong talons. An adult snowy owl can eat between three and five lemmings every day.

Female snowy owls' feathers are speckled, which makes them difficult to spot on the ground where they make their nests.

female snowy owl

chick

Snowy owls mate for life. They meet up each summer to mate and raise their young.

The chicks' feathers also help them to hide from animals such as Arctic foxes and large seabirds, which will try to eat them. If a chick is attacked, the parent owls will dive-bomb the attackers to drive them away.

Unlike many other owls, burrowing owls are active in the daytime. They nest in burrows underground. Often they take over abandoned burrows dug by other animals, but they can dig their own burrows if they need to.

burrowing owl

chick

Burrowing owls have the longest legs of any owl.

If burrowing owl chicks are disturbed, they make a sound like a rattle snake to scare off their predators (the animals that want to eat them).

Burrowing owls collect dung and put it around the entrance to their burrow. Then they sit very still and wait. The dung attracts dung beetles, which burrowing owls think are yummy to eat. Burrowing owls also eat lizards, birds, rodents and other insects.

When a burrowing owl is alarmed, it jerks its body up and down.

dung

Meet the smallest owl: the elf owl. Elf owls have a loud voice, and they make high-pitched whistles and squeaks.

At just 14cm tall, elf owls are about the same size as a can of fizzy drink, and they have a wingspan of only 26cm!

At night, elf owls hunt moths, crickets, centipedes, beetles and other insects by listening for them. They do not need to drink because they get everything they need to live from the insects they eat.

Elf owls live in hot desert habitats. They live in America in summer, but in winter they fly to Mexico because the American desert gets too cold for them!

cactus hole nest

Elf owls nest high up in holes in trees or cactuses. They often use old woodpecker holes. Having a nest high up helps protect the elf owl from hungry predators, such as other owls, snakes and bobcats. If elf owls are threatened, they pretend to be dead and hope that the predator will go away.

Eagle owls are the biggest owls at 75cm tall, with a wingspan of 188cm.

eagle owl

Eagle owls tend to live in high, lonely mountains and build their nests on the edges of cliffs. They lay two eggs three days apart so that their chicks hatch at different times.

chick

Owl chicks are called owlets.

When an eagle owl is annoyed, it clicks its bill and spits, lowers its head, ruffles its back feathers, fans out its tail and spreads out its wings.

an annoyed eagle owl

It might look like owls can turn their heads all the way around, but in fact they can only turn their heads ¾ of the way around.

Barn owls are one of the commonest owls. They are often seen hunting across farmland and along the sides of roads.

barn owl

mouse

Like other owls, barn owls make no noise as they fly. The animals they hunt do not know they are there until it is too late!

Like eagle owls, barn owls also lay their eggs two or three days apart. The number of eggs and young that survive depends on how much food is available. If food is short, the youngest or weakest chick might die. However, if there is plenty of food and good weather, a pair could raise two broods.

barn owl chick

Barn owls often nest in old buildings, but they will also nest in holes in trees or in the nest boxes that have been put up to attract them.

adult owl

chick

Tawny owls live in woodland. They get their name from their tawny brown feathers.

Not all owls say 'twit-twoo', but tawny owls do. In fact, the 'twit-twoo' is made up of two calls: the female says 'twit' (or /kee-wick/) and the male responds with 'hoo, hoo'.

Tawny owls pair for life. They nest in holes in trees, and they defend their territory aggressively.

Tawny owls are nocturnal and hunt small mammals, mice and rats. They glide noiselessly down from their perch to grab their victims.

owl pellet

fur

bone

Like other owls, tawny owls eat by gulping an animal down whole. Then all of the 'bits', such as fur, bones, teeth and feathers are regurgitated (vomited up) in pellets. These owl pellets can be found on the ground under nesting and roosting sites. Owl pellets can be cut up to see what the owl has eaten.

Like the burrowing owl, the northern hawk owl is active in the daytime. Northern hawk owls often look like hawks when they are flying.

northern hawk owl

In summer, northern hawk owls mainly eat mammals, but in the winter they also eat birds, such as ptarmigan and grouse. A northern hawk owl can detect an animal even if it is under thick snow. The owl will plunge up to a foot into the snow to catch whatever is there.

Northern hawk owls nest in the tops of the hollow stumps of dead trees. The female sits on the eggs, while the male hunts for food. About two weeks after the chicks have hatched, the female starts to leave the nest so that she can hunt. The male stays on the nest and guards the owlets while she is away.

northern hawk owl guarding nest

As is the case with many types of owl, the female northern hawk owl is bigger than the male.

Little owls are the smallest owls found in the UK. They are quite common, and can often be seen perching on a tree in the daytime. Little owls nest in holes in dead trees and old buildings.

little owl chicks

little owl

Little owls eat small mammals, birds, beetles and other insects. They have very good eyesight, and can see at night as well as in the daytime. They hunt at dusk and can often be seen running along the ground after small animals and insects.